Little Fires

Beth Bentley

Cune

Seattle
1998

Copies of *Little Fires* are available in paperback for $15.95 plus $2.50 shipping and handling within the United States. ($1.50 shipping and handling for each additional book.)

Individuals: To order, visit our online bookstore (www.cunepress.com). Or call (800) 789-7055. Or email to Cune@cunepress.com. Or send a check to Cune, P.O. Box 31024, Seattle, WA 98103. Washington State residents add 8.6 % sales tax.

Bookstores: Cune Press books are available from Bookpeople, Baker & Taylor, Ingram, and Koen.

Cune is a project of the Allied Arts Foundation. You are welcome to make tax-deductible contributions to "Cune Project/Allied Arts" and mail to Cune at the above address. For information about Cune books, send a note to the above address or email Books@cunepress.com. To schedule Cune authors for readings or interviews, call (206) 789-7055. Contact Cune by fax: (206) 782-1330; or email: Cune @cunepress.com. Visit our online magazine: http://www.cunepress.com

The Local/International Series
Cune is an online magazine and literary press based in Seattle. We operate as an artists and writers cooperative and publish "local writers of international significance."

Contents

For Nelson, Sean, and Julian

"Alors, seulement quand elle l'a éclairé, quand elle l'a intellectualisé, on distingue, et avec quelle peine, la figure de ce qu'on a senti."

Marcel Proust

"And is not this work of spontaneous recollection, in which remembrance is the woof and forgetting the warp, a counterpart to Penelope's work rather than its likeness?"

Walter Benjamin

I

A Victorian Girlhood

It was not as if she ever perceived
the "either" or "or" as she emerged
to the lake's sparkling surface,
glisteningly fresh, as if water
were all of the world, her lucent
extension, without encumbrances,
the unnecessary alternatives of
east or west beaches, grass islands
or rafts; floated there feeling
happily expected (since there were no
accidents then, only the inevitable's
curtain stuck on its rod, unable
to move back or forth).

              She assumed
the same lack of choices, drifting
not quite aware of or even rebelling
against want of a tide. The suitors came,
one at a time. You can see them
in old photographs, rare to be sure,
she pressed against his hard shoulder
like a lily caught on an oar; then
in her Egyptian dancer's outfit, posed
as a figure on a frieze, a formal attitude,
though it seems to imply, if not embody,
the physical, that is, the expectation
of joy. How did it all drift away?

The dogdays thickened, weeds clustered.
They loved those large family picnics,
tables foundering with food, followed

by naps or chases through the woods
where panting encounters resulted
in necessary though conveniently dynastic
mergers. When did she decide just to stay
where she was, treading water and nervously
screaming for help, never turning
in the cold flood to kick up her heels,
set out for the shadowy distant
but solid real estate on the shore?

Dorothy

Alone. Made pies and stuffed a pike. Baked a loaf.
Headache after dinner. I lay down.
A note from Wm. roused me. Tied up scarlet beans.
Letters to C. and Mary. Nailed up the honeysuckles.
On Rydale Lake a boat floating by itself upon the water.
The horned moon gave lovely light from Dunmail Raise.

My Beloved home, composing in the orchard.
Coleridge arrived alone, eyes swollen from the wind.
He seemed half-stupefied. Read poems on the water.
Let the boat take its own course. Toothache. Slept
in Wm.'s bed. Felt better. Made a shoe. Letters from Mary and Sara.
Wm. walked poor Coleridge back to Keswick.

Baking day. Little loaves. Copied out Wm.'s poems.
Swallows, dear loves, hanging on the panes,
white bellies and forked tails like fish. Letters
to C. and Mary. Walked alone to Ambleside.
Wm. sadly tired. Threatening piles, headache
from composing. Moon like yellow cornfields on Rydale water.

In John's Grove, we lay in a trench, listening to waterfalls
and birds, no one waterfall above another. Wm.'s eyes closed.
Ached with the sound of water in the air,
the voice of the air. A lovely coolness over us.
Wm. brought me the only glowworm in the orchard.
C.'s letter made me melancholy. I eased my heart by weeping.

Baked a giblet pie. Put books in order. No letters. Home by Clappersgate.
Watered the garden. Columbines on the rocks. Here and there
a lone one shaded by Tufts and Bowers
of trees. Wm. pillowed on my shoulder. The single columbine,
a slender, lovely creature, a female seeking retirement,

growing freest and most graceful when most alone. Headache.

Ten o'clock. I write with aching heart to Coleridge.
A quiet night. The fire flutters. The watch ticks. Letters
to Mary and Sara. I hear nothing but the Breathing of my Beloved
as now and then he pushes his book forward and turns a leaf. Rainwater
hissing in the chimney. Wm. sighs. I hear the owls hoot
in the trees outside. A lonely sparrow chirps on the roof.

Letters done. I leave Wm. Take my aching body to bed
alone. Water too cold to wash. My tooth broke. They will soon
be gone. No matter. I will be beloved. I want no more.

* A concealed sestina

The Alphabet at Harar

"Je ne me crois pas embarqué pour une noce avec Jésus Christ pour beau-père."

Arthur Rimbaud

Nothing. I changed nothing.
Grotesque exaggerations of the soul.
Cords of my spirit twanged off-key,
then broke. A green boy turned handsprings
on a lawn of nails to amuse the grown-ups.
He willed new gods of stone and wire,
an offering of shrunken heads
to clack in the wind. Sly games.

The men in hats still promenade,
a quadrille of consonants. I'm
the thin mongrel at the door, the runt
of the litter. I've eaten everything,
become my disease. I ate
my heart and puked it,
then lapped it up again.

Anger's Iroquois, red-eyed,
I thought the sun would bleach me.
How far away the birds and fountains,
my dear vowels, are.

Ha ha, I'm *en famille* once more,
mother, sister, priest, black skirts,
a circle of stinking holes.

Water, child's voice, where are you?
Visions? The white, the green, the white
blue green diapason.

My old spouses settled down,
sober and impotent;
the boy in me stays shrill.

I'll make my knees pay for their cowardice.
I've reached my O,
O emptiness.

My rot smells like violets.

Eurydice's Version

1

Well, I wasn't always alone, you see. There were those—
how shall I name them?—not like us; some limbed,
some not. Difficult to say, since they were never still,
never completely visible. Nor were they even the same

from one moment to the next, and not like one another, either:
visages like candles or rocks, that is, full of light
or opaque: they hovered. It was their eyes that
signalled lively possibilities. Not that I could see them,

no, but they were presences; they followed or encircled me,
they closed or opened like hands, like hands came forward,
grasped or repulsed, were cold or warm. Without voices,
of course, for that would be absurd—talking eyes,

as we say, one of our fictions. No. I simply felt
them there or not there. But never as the eyes
of friends or enemies, not that kind of touching.
In fact, there was no touching at all—

except as one might sense the thin, hard edge
of a fingernail that pushes a drugged insect
to see its underside or watch its antennae wave.
Perhaps I was wrong to think those eyes benign.

2

Songs aren't worth much here.
I told him that,
but he wouldn't listen,
believing in his own
invincibility like a child.
They're not much interested

in bodies, either, they've
so many of them—everyone
thinks his is the best.

It's pathetic the way
people present perfect legs and arms,
breasts wrapped in tissue like roses.
And then to see them turned down
or, at best, offered a pittance!
All those fine reflexes, carefully nurtured,
and for what? No,
it is the invisible we sniff around,
something that can't be touched or tasted.

Perhaps we sense a pulse the way
a witching rod senses water,
below tons of earth, moving.
I say "we," having become
a minor servant, something like
a kitchen-maid sorting vegetables.
As for Orpheus, they hear him,
truly, but not his breathing,
not his songs.

3
Voices? Voices, you ask, as if
it were not voices we evade.

How they follow us, ricocheting
from wall to wall, interminably

rhythmic. Days when lyrics
fall with the monotonous

regularity of rain. If we could only
not talk, not hear, the solitude

would be bearable. If there were sounds
without words, swelling

like water or clouds, greening
the corridors, filling the throat.

We are drowning here, under
an avalanche of delineations.

We are garroted, hands tangled
in masses of syllables.

Language has found its way
down to the deepest place

where we cannot pillow our ears
from it, even by dying.

4
For years your voice crouched
in the hallways of my thought,
assassin or guardian, never
completely concealed, though
master of disguises. Our encounters
at the elevator were no more poignant
than your whisper behind the shower curtain.
Nursemaid of my life, strong dog,
even in exile I heard the murmur
of your anxiety and resolution.

What sonnets you built out of
the tears I lent you. Finally, across

the chasm of double worlds
you threw your voice like ectoplasm,
confident it would net me
out of deep waters. But saw
your own face in those waters.
Your loose hand let me slip
so far down, tons of ocean drown
even the echo of your echo.

The Country Boy

In memory of Theodore Roethke

Was it their voices
riding the family range
from baritone to soprano,
humming like bees,
that pulled you from room to room
hunting for treasure?

It seemed a safe, aimless sound,
hardly a tune,
and you either followed it
or it followed you on your rounds,
until you knew each other by heart.

The screen on the door orchestrated sooty overtures
to the fly on the grid,
a counterpoint in blue.
Or the rain talked to the windows
about something darker outside.

Later they found you stunned
before the impassive rectitude of winter,
knee-deep in stillness,
as if chained to the fence,
before you shook yourself and laughed
and, to everyone's relief,
made the snow sing the song you had made for it.

In spring the creek elucidated
what the faucets had merely implied.
You crawled closer on bruised knees.
Alone or not alone, there was nothing

to do but listen.
There were all those questions
only the grass could answer.

Though nothing was free;
you proffered your temperature
like a barefooted man hoping for shoes,
striking bargains.

They thought you might start a fire
in the dry fields, or break the stalks
on one of your headlong plunges.
The tinder under your coat
and the noise, that by now
none of them could avoid hearing,
made them uneasy.

Was the house glad when you left?
The attic, strewn with the bones
of nestlings and mice,
didn't believe in tears.
Downstairs the old one whispered,
"Wind's rising."
They fastened the shutters.

A Desperate Enthusiasm

"The root of your error . . . is the slightinge of God's Faythfull
Ministers and contemninge and cryinge down them as
Nobodies."

Rev. John Wilson, Church of Boston

"Aye, it is the most desperate enthusiasm in the world . . .
I'm persuaded that the revelation she brings forth is
delusion . . ."

Gov. John Winthrop

"Better to be cast out of the Church than to deny Christ."

Anne Hutchinson, March 26, 1638
Testimony before the Great and
General Court of Massachusetts

Boston's ice'd over. Ships fix'd in the bay
   moan like cattle haunch-high in mud.
     Masts rattle and clash
  in winter's war; the air's strange.
   At Spring Gate the women bite their lips for fear
    some minister might hear my name.

We fast and freeze, no fuel for our grates nor our hearts.
   I'm fix'd, too, in Mistress Weld's
    dark foreroom. Does God speak?
  I'm deaf. Last week Hett's wife
   went distract'd and threw her baby
    in the well. Then Dorothy Talbye

fall'n into a melancholy slew her infant daughter.

We're in a blast'd place, punisht
   I think. John Cotton,
I'm unvisited by you.
   The men you will not raise your voice
      against bully and bait me.

I go mad, turning my head this way
   and that, a wounded she-bear tortur'd
      to despair. Zealous
   Symmes, thinking to trick me
      into rash speech, and Peters in a corner
         scribbling notes. Dark men

smiling with clos'd lips on broken teeth.
   Their bloodless hands stay in their pockets
      as if to touch were to burn.
   Shepherd, whom all call
      sweet-natur'd, thinks questions vil'st errors
         but questions me till my mind shrieks.

Weld worries the rag-ends of my sanity
   like a dog with a shoe. John, where are you?
      Mononotto's wife
and the captured Pequod women
   dam the High Street wailing for their men.
      Should I mourn my once-trust'd Mentor?

My sweet Will visits. And Edward, Bridget, Faith
   know their mother's true, though she's
      forbidd'n to instruct them.

My shawl's a widow's cowl.
　　At night I pace my confines and brood
　　　　on Mary Dyer's stillborn Thing

that Goody Hawkins and I pull'd out in gobbets:
　　I didn't count its arms and legs
　　　　You counsell'd me
　　to have it buried unseen.
　　　　Now rumors fly like blackbirds from house
　　　　　　to house; they hang in the trees.

But Edward's Katherine birthed Elishua whole:
　　my first grandchild: God is my salvation. John,
　　　　Bishop Aylmer call'd my father
　　"Overthwart proud Puritan knave,"
　　　　and cried, "Have him to Marshalsea!"
　　　　　　"I am to go whither it pleaseth God,"

Father answer'd. John, I'm Marbury's daughter!
　　I follow'd you to Boston. Now
　　　　a company of legal
　　professors lie poring o'er the laws
　　　　which Christ abolisht. They come to me
　　　　　　in private, but save my words

like crumbs, their sliding codfish eyes white
　　and hypocritical. The fear of man
　　　　's a snare. Why should I
　　be afraid? I'm candid. Christ's hand
　　　　holds mine. In Boston souls slip under
　　　　　　the ice. Will spring resurrect them?

Vane's shipp'd back to England like a bad boy,
   Coddington and Coggershall silence'd by the magistrates,
      and you want to please
   all sides. Soft-spoken John.
      In Winthrop's town Winthrop dictates
         the law; he prosecutes and judges.

Tom Oliver says there's a hard thing in my womb
   though I'm past child-bearing. It grows apace.
      Is't monster or blessing?
   Is it my sorrow? Is it the harsh names
   call'd me; heretic, seducer, leper?
      I cramp with pain. John,

you should've voted for the veil, women unseen as well
   as unheard. I'm not Mistress Bradstreet. I cannot
      rhyme, but must utter:
   I see Boston plain, though my window's
   glaz'd over; there's disease in her womb. Let the Lord
      judge. Christ's giv'n me His Seal.

Schiele in Prison

As usual, you escaped, hop
like a magician, Father,
out of your box and hiding
somewhere offstage; inside
the coffin, frail as an after-
birth, pullulates
the milky substance of your son.

Now the state finds I fit
these walls—all pock-marks and
syphilitic boils. They burnt
my paintings just as you did—
remember those childish trains?
You taught me to prefer the body's
engines: little sister and I

honeymooned in Trieste like you
and Mother. Nothing to look at
here except each other. My mirror
sends your eyes back, crazy and mean.
I paint us all hands and genitals,
eating ourselves, while the squint
that is God looks on.

Grotesque mates, our doubles
multiply, until even my palette's
children reflect the twitch of us
in their rachitic bones. I lock
the family into this frame,
mortise the corners. Presto, change-o!
It's the world!

Arachne

She took the green whip of childhood,
wrapped it around the pin of her fear
       and knotted it at the center.

She took the rusty chain of her bloodline,
looped it over the marrow of her grief,
       and knotted it at the center.

She took the lithe reins of her sexuality,
tightened them on the nail of solitude,
       and knotted them at the center.

She took the silk of her mother's lie,
secured it on the thumb of her contempt,
       and knotted it at the center.

She took the ripple of her father's shrug,
turned it twice on the spit of her skill,
       and knotted it at the center.

Gathering the veins of her inflexible will,
she twisted them into a noose,
       and hoisted herself into its center.

When light uncoiled from the spool of her being
she was reborn on the limb of the tensile
       counterpoised in the center.

Emily

(July 30, 1818–December 19, 1848)

"I am Heathcliff."

Cathy, *Wuthering Heights*

"The soul to feel the flesh, the flesh to feel the chain."

October 9, 1845

"... l'universe me paraissait une vaste machine con-
struit seulement pour produit le mal."

Le Papillon, Brussels, 1842

1
At school the stone floors sweated death;
mold flourished on the wall by my bed.
I reached out to touch it, thinking
it would smell like the moor's rocks
gloved in moss. I wanted to put
my cheek there, only
the starved ghosts of my dead sisters
rattled the windows and the smell
was their sour breath on the sheets.
I took a chill I wore for years,
a cold finger on my neck. After that
all houses other than my own stank
like open graves. I side-stepped them
and held my breath, deaf to the passing-bell.

2
Once I lived in a town where the birds
spoke a foreign language. God knows,
I tried to love the flowers.

Poor things, they had female
souls and adored their boxes.
Even the storms were stunted
and went roaring down dead streets
like the English playing skittles,
harmless in the end. They petered out.
Like me, in that place. I contained
my cries, my rage slid round
the empty room of my heart,
a crippled animal that'd
found a hole to die in.

3

In Brussels, Charlotte loved a man,
or thought she did, or thought he was one.
There were words and looks. His wife
vibrato'd on the taut string of her nerves.
But I recorded emptiness, rooms
the souls had fled from, passion
hanging limp, a wet petticoat
in the windless yard of their minds.
I thought of that gloat of thunder
exulting across our hills, and the tree
by the waterfall, cleft one night
into two trees, broken but living.
In pallid sun, my sister's pruned plant
splayed like a dwarf, large head a'loll.

4

When Charlotte woke me the night
she smelled smoke, I was dreaming:
I was in Hell—it was Brussels in darkness:

rumbling carriage-wheels, a smother of dust,
faces masked under a glaze of yellow.
I wasn't afraid—it appeared familiar.
And when I hastened to drag
poor Branwell from his smouldering sheets
the smell of fire seemed natural.
It was natural to have charred hands
and stinging eyes. Frail and limp as a savaged
fox, his body, his white face quenched in its
frenzy of red hair I thought of Absalom.
Father's fear of fire scorched us all.

5
Sometimes in the churchyard, I read names:
we live with the dead: Maria, Elizabeth,
the mother they say had me—
flattened under slabs. I sit on stones
and peruse the closed book of families.
By the parsonage the thwarted limbs
of hawthorn scribble fleshless stories.
I'm thorny, too, and lean, practicing
invisibility. No meat
on our table or our bones.
All the lighter to dance on graves, my dears,
gay as Aunt Branwell, bonnet nodding
to the brisk tap of her cherished small feet
in the lost parlors of Cornwell.

6

Boyish, the fat quail of Keighley pronounce.
I hide a smile. I love my hard legs.
I rise before Tabby, scrub and iron,
then over three stiles and onto the moors, with Keeper.
I contend with sharpest rocks, goat-shameless,
scrabbling. Waves, waves, an ocean
of hills petalling out, I
the calyx of that dark rose. The witty rain
licks off my mask, air's an antidote
to the disease of towns. My athletic soul
climbs above peat bogs, above Keighley
cannibal'd under its plague of factory smoke—
eating, being eaten—until I've lost earth,
I'm healed hawk, whole-winged.

7

Kittens in a weighted sack, we women
drown, scarcely complaining. But when man
abdicates, we're shocked.
Once Father cured impatience firing
his revolver through the window, scattering
cats and maids. Now he totters
under the wind and hail of Branwell's
mad barrage. And Branwell borrows
sovereigns from the kitchen funds
pretending to pay debts, but spends it

of an evening at the Black Bull, buying
courage, friends, inches, will.
Will's expensive, Faith beyond our means.

8

"Waiting Boy" was Anne's man, mine
"Grave-y"—the Major has her
serious side. But I don't let
toys lead me. It's the rising
I try for, like my bread on the warm stove
summer mornings. It inflates, my hands
punch it down, it rises up, I shape it—
there's more to bread than air.
But who would trust another's hands?
Is it wrong not to love harshness?
The stone-cutter chip chips
the music I've grown used to. I have
my will. I can choose
to choose my way of falling.

9

They say old Grimshaw whipped
sinners out of the Black Bull Sundays
and into chapel. Father
chose not to see, until, in truth,
his eyes clouded. Now
it's late, late and the boy's
lost, body infected with soul's
sores, uncauterized. The Sicilian
pea and crimson cornflower wasted here,
too gaudy, too delicate for our soil—

they couldn't bear dryness.
Branwell, manikin, to pull yourself upright
the last minute, and for whose sake? I turn
from light that does not warm, but burns.

10
The place I left, secret, except
to small slip-soft creatures, I won't
get back to. Never mind. My hand
pressed its star there; the stream
says *Emily, Emily*.
The house is my mistress this short
last while, though shut windows
never held thought in. The body's house
loosens, it'll scatter soon, a tumbled
barn, letting in air and birds.
Snow, be quick. Astonish my bones:
I want to be re-invented.
Mother me back to absolute coolness,
small hands. I'm fever. Quell me.

II

Posthumous Letters

Suspense at Meran

*October 2, 1923: ". . . and the evil powers, whether on good
or bad assignments, were only lightly fingering the entrances
through which they were going to penetrate someday, an
event to which they were already looking forward with
unbearable rejoicing."*

*October 23, 1923: ". . . But there is a certain justice in being
associated with the fate of Germany, like you and me."*

Franz Kafka, *Letters to Max Brod*

Max, someone wrote me that when the mob
paused at Father's store, a man yelled,
"Not Kafka, he's all right!" And they ran on
to smash the windows of some other Jew.
I suppose it's because he speaks Czech
or has Czech employees. Certainly
not because he's kind.
Here in Meran, in the dining-room,
I sit with two old ladies and a general
and a colonel—all Christians.
They're interested in my name
and because I come from Prague.
So it begins. You're Czech? No?
German-Bohemian, then? The Little Quarter?
The general has the German true blue
military eyes. He looks me over.
Finally, I confess—is that the word, Max?
Or admit?—I am a Jew.

The entire dining-room falls silent.
Not even the clink of a fork.
Jackdaw or raven. It's a matter
of language, Max. Kafka
by any other name—but our destinies
are linked, the general and I.
I'm the only one he can talk to.

We read the same books, more or less.
We're a sort of intellectual élite—
until we leave the sanitorium;
after all, one has to talk to someone
in these hell-holes.
But all of us are amiable, though some
are drowning. No one has the bad taste
to drown in public.
We graze on each other
though I'm a thorn in their flesh,
the nettle in their craws.

The general is my father-judge;
under his kindness he wears
a leather belt; his blue eyes
are noncommittal as a bullet.
Don't ask me to move, Max.
The moving of a chair
disturbs my equilibrium.
This fear's the final fear.
Let me stay put. When have I not been poised, an inept apprentice,
between the fear of action

and the fear of death?
The devil loves me because I write.
The dining-room's a restful purgatory.

Note: "Kavka" is the Czech word for "Jackdaw." "Jakovke" is the Yiddish word for "Jacob." In 1788, when the Jews were allowed to adopt German surnames, Kafka's family chose instead to adopt a Czech name.

Degrees of White

*September 1917: "Sometimes it seems to me that my brains
and my lungs came to an agreement without my knowledge.
"Things can't go on this way," said the brain, and after five
years the lungs said they were ready to help."*

Kafka, *Letters to Max Brod*

The white is white as far as the eye can see,
though troughs and gullies deepen to a purplish hue
that reminds him of boiled milk or the sly cast

of shadows on a body so thin all the bones
are ridges. Since it's before dawn he's in silence
and alone on heights that for the moment show

no tracks but his, and this desired and unnatural
emptiness is like the space one enters
between consciousness and dream before the blank

is written on, in whatever colored ink.
He surveys a sheet that he can crawl beneath
or skim, weightless, leaving no trace. He listens

to the whistle of his lungs the doctor calls
his "music," a personal cantata. It blends
with voices from the distance that pierce his glaze

the way bird-calls shiver windows after
a *nuit-blanche,* horrible and welcome:
they score his solitude, the circle of waste.

Afterwords: Felicia

*October 25, 1923: "I do not trust words and letters, my words
and letters; I want to share my heart with people but not
with phantoms that play with words and read the letters with
slavering tongue."*

Kafka, *Letters to Max Brod*

Certainly I should have known our lives
would only jar each other,
two croquet balls that hit with a smack
and then shoot off in different directions.

You entered the room like a burglar,
slid along the wall, and then
sat all evening foraging with eyes
dark and tight as purses,
spending nothing.

We're different species, Franz,
bloods that, mingled, would have produced
monsters. Still,
you made the move. It was you,
your aggression that brought us close.
You had some fixed design
burnt onto your brain,
a punishing dream: Marry! Marry!

And so the game began. Over six hundred letters!
As if you could only love with words.
They poured their sweet and sour
over me until I was engulfed.
The pale soul I was

disappeared in that deluge;
all you could taste was your own dire concoction.

You opened your veins to show me
every cell, rooms of light and dark,
fresh-smelling or rotten.

Then stood before the castle door,
caretaker, refusing entrance.

Do you remember our walk around the pond
near Tetschen-Bodenbach, where the black swan
sailed so near we could see his eye's red rim
and his bill like a bloody knife?
I dreamt of him that night, dreamt
he beaked me to shreds,
screaming all the while.

The next day you grew quiet,
silent as stone, darker,
more saturnine as time went on.
But dragged our feelings out,
unravelling the garment of our love
year upon year;

until, with what relief
you hemorrhaged the whole affair.
And it was nothing but black string,
a tangle of alphabet.

When I married elsewhere
I relieved you of guilt, of the obligation
to be the father instead of the son,

while you looked for a mother among
acquaintances, playing hide-and-go-seek

to the end. Your family kept the funeral
private, though that girl was there, the last one.
Did she feel your leathery feet on her skin,
your icy thighs?
When your throat was so ravaged you couldn't speak
and your pen was stilled, then
did you open your wings?

As for me, a long, black indelible
thread of despair
weaves through my wilderness of blood
and keens for a conjugate call.

Undelivered Mail

November 1919: "Sometimes I imagine the map of the world spread out and you stretched diagonally across it. And I feel as if I could consider living in only those regions that either are not covered by you or not within your reach."

Kafka, *Letter to His Father*

Writing about them is no cure;
we want to hold out our bruises, see,
it's still here, years later, the discoloration.
Even after they've gone, forgetful, into death,
we're stuck with remembering;
we tongue the exposed nerve
to reassure ourselves it still hurts.

It's the good we remember that traps us,
the praise we hear about second-hand,
or the ambiguous gift that sends us the message,
"This is the kind of person I'd like you to be."

How to separate in the churn of glamour
love from rage?
Or is that the curse, Franz?
Our fathers, our mothers,
huge skin-forms we crawl inside,
children in grown-ups' clothing,
macabre, flopping about.

We have the gift of language
because all our retorts are muffled,
driven inward.
We're swollen with diseased cells.

When at last words spill out,
sometimes amazing us, having learned
in their sanitorium a kind of
beautiful efficiency,
the soul's tongue is still tied.

Malnourished, the child sits
under a frail umbrella,
gazing upward at the clever giant
whose shadow is a sheet of driving rain,
black wings, a mourning garment,
a ravenous hole.

Posthumous Letters

April 1921: "There is only a single disease, no more, and medicine blindly chases down this one disease as though hunting a beast in endless forests."

Kafka, *Letters to Max Brod*

Everything about you is history:
your fate is grafted to ours,
an errant limb. Your uncertainties
invade our cells, inherited weakness.
We remember the way you lay on your bed
in an ecstasy of self-loathing,
and we adopt your element, despair.

We cultivate it in our minds
where it spreads its convictions from a suitable height
to waiting admirers
who will snow the city with campaign literature
in exquisite taste.

How we court apathy, the paralyzed runner,
and his sibling, devilish innocence,
with her inadequate breasts and a stammer—
characters in the morality play
that is performed in a vacant lot
once occupied by church or synagogue:
bricks lie scattered and twists of lead
from melted stained-glass windows.

You are our modern hero,
sick and single, a Hamlet,
whose father, analphabetic, coarse and strong,

outlives him. You sought
the one true religion, language,
and rode its inevitabilities
from spa to spa, spurred on
by your premonitions of a quelled voice
and the last diaspora.

III

Young Pale Boy

In the west three geese
stroke green on the sky
because their wings tell them
to dream of water.

     His eyes seed the frosted air
     with rain-colored questions.

Rain invites the hawthorn leaves
to have their cheeks read.

     The child's long bones whisper
     in their silk house.

Air, the nubile leaves,
blink into season.

     He leans against the telephone pole
     outside the junior high,
     cigarette not much thinner
     nor whiter than his fingers.

At the street's end, the chestnut
bellows in splendid baritone.

     His crescent cheek-bones refuse
     to calendar the weather.

The wind posts the breath of Green Lake,
writes the names of flowers in Latin.

     His mouth canoes in a clear lake.

It is not for the school-bell
to color the afternoon.

    His white throat,

for which there is no metaphor,
vaults from his collar.

The Pastry Maker

Wherever we come from, we're moons:
we enter the brown lake of the shop
from light. Light behind us, light
reflected on our foreign faces,
light in our smiles toward her shadow
behind the counter, where even the pastries
in their fluted skirts are serious.
We taste the damaged fruit of her eyes.

What does she see? She sees
just enough. Her thick, soft body
bends, a trained beast, docile
in clothes that bind it. She peers
at my daughter beside me, a princess
whose tanned cheeks breathe luck. Behind glasses
her magnified pupils read
our aura of happy endings.

But we've seen her on a Sunday street
in the watercolor radiance of Paris,
with her mother and a young man whose red hand
is massive on her arm, whose face
says country. She lets them guide her, smiling.

I see her smiling in a stone house where
her large frame fits large furniture.
Her touch takes her from bedroom to kitchen.
She strokes blue cups, an iron skillet,
intimate as her own breasts and belly.
Lets warmth lead her outside, through edges
of sunlight, toward the sweet pierce of hay
and manure, where the barn floats shimmering.

She enters the dominion of shadow, and sits
resting her head against the warm flank
of a cow. Her cheeks drink morning.

Eyes closed behind steel-rimmed glasses,
she reaches, cups the soft, heavy udders.
Her hands tense, then open. She pulls,
lets go, pulls, head pressing the creature.

She enters its life, absorbed
in the book of the senses, the animal
braille, blood's dream. It unfolds,
calm as the lake in the depth of her own slow body.

Marcel

Sometimes by the water's edge
we come to what Papa calls
"pleasure houses," and a girl
leans over the bank, trailing her hand in;
she's pliant as a trout. I imagine
fishing with her, casting our lines
toward blue irises. She smells
of water and fresh-cut grass. I dream
that I am swimming and the river
turns blue-black, changing color
like the stained-glass chapel window
of Gilbert the Bad. The current twists me,
rolling me over. There's someone swimming
with me, his body's strong and so close
I can hardly breathe. He presses down
and presses down. And then we're running,
he's chasing me, I'm chasing him,
we're at a table in the garden
drinking out of tall thin glasses
something white that Papa says
is bad for me. I cough so hard
it makes me gasp. I jerk awake
to damp sheets and the smell of salt.

Mornings, I see pink light through my eyelids,
Françoise is downstairs talking. When
I find her in the garden, she's shaking
a chicken by the head and yelling
"Nasty bird!" It scares me. Her right hand
holds the axe. The kitchen-maid
weeps while she peels asparagus.

They're slim and cool and green-tipped
shading to blue and mauve. When I crunch one
even the dirt tastes good. She puts them
in little rows like soldiers. The maid
moans and holds her stomach. Her big dress
hides the part the baby's in. She smells
of sweat and vegetables and lard.

In the meadow I look back at the spires
of St. Hilaire's pointing to the sky,
faint as pencil strokes on sketching paper.
I follow a path to where the hawthorns are,
and put my face among pink rosettes.
When I force one open with my little finger
it's all red inside like the cat's mouth.
A bracelet of red beads circles my wrist
where the thorns bit me. The little girl
I dreamed would write me tender letters
stood behind the fence and stared. She raised
her hand and made a rude sign. I thought
of all the bad things I could shout
if I felt like it, but then somebody called her.
Her eyes are sly as Theodore's.
In bed I think of her crisp red hair
and the freckles like pink coins on her cheeks.
We ride together on a pony, her arms
around my waist. She rubs against me
and we both fall off. She's lying on top
of me, her chest's on mine, she's close
as the actress I met at uncle's house,
she was so pretty in her pink silk dress

and pearls, she smiled and took
my face between her hands and said
I looked like Papa. Uncle frowned.
Mama didn't and didn't come. I counted
to one hundred, then cried and fell asleep.

At Montjouvain the pond at sunset
was so still I could see the pink
roof tiles reflected in it, clear
enough to count. I felt so happy
I jumped up and down. "Hey, hey,
hey, hey!" I yelled, and shook my umbrella
at the sky. It was so cool I fell
asleep behind the doctor's house
and when I woke up it was dark
and I could see inside. The room
was light and motionless like those
glass jars the boys put under water
to catch live minnows in. The doctor's
daughter and her girlfriend seemed
to swim in clearness back and forth,
slowly touching and kissing. Then the friend
spit on the doctor's photograph
and pulled the daughter onto the couch.
She wept, then ran to close the shutters.
They were quiet. I ran home.

Some days the river's darker. Tadpoles
explode like stars. Tap, tap, the rain
hits lily pads. When I gaze in
I see my face brown and green

shifting mysteriously. I feel
myself pulled down. A slow garden
of thin plants reaches up, catching
my hair and hands. Another boy
looks back at me. Our mouths touch,
I dream of Mama and she doesn't
recognize me and hurries along
a corridor with people I don't know.
I follow her, then see that it
is Theodore looking around
over his shoulder and smiling the way
he does when he plays a trick.
I'm panting after, Mama's watching us
from the upstairs bedroom window,
the doctor's with her. My chest hurts.
The maid's dress is smothering me,
I'm underneath it, I'm between
her knees. I try to cry out, "Mama, mama!"
but my words are muffled, I can only
moan. She doesn't hear me, she's gone off,
and I don't know
if I'm asleep or drowned.

Beaux Arts

The elderly gentleman,
upright and finger-spare
in the black glove of his suit,
slid casually
during the andante cantabile
from seat 26, row K
to the sound-proofed floor,
sinking without a murmur
in Meany Hall's vast twilight,
with the ease of a pen
that slips unheeded
from a relaxed hand
to embed itself in the carpet.

And two other gentlemen,
similarly clad,
bent over him
and, after a moment's hesitation,
raised his loosely-jointed form
that shifted, slack
as odd-sized sticks of kindling
in a gunny-sack,
and carried him swiftly along
row K, where people rose
in a shadowy arc like a wave
that washes up the shore
and then subsides
so fast you are not sure
whether the tide's
incoming or outgoing;
while the musicians go on bowing

as they move
into poco piu adagio and the finale
"without a break,
that finds Beethoven in his
sunny mood with a quirk-
y main theme that trips
along happily
accompanied by staccato
figurations and punctuations
of sharp sforzandos."

In the Hotel Garden

The din of traffic, guests
eddying through gates:
apart, the old couple
folding sheets.

The white fabric billows,
lengthens into a silken ripple
across which they survey each other
as one squints down a road
at an approaching friend.

They are private, linked
in the act of holding,
hands engaged in texture that
tents them in freshness.
It flaps, rolls, a mild wake
between them, a contained sea.

The white cotton sheet gathers
the August afternoon, the sun's slant
over the magnolias, their granddaughter's
bicycle leaning against the wall.

It invites them to a slow dance:
they bring the four corners together,
step back, forward, back,
turning and folding, a doing
that is in itself complete.

The four old hands meet, touch, part.
The sheet ruffles its white wings.
This continues.

For Sally in Paris

So now it is he who's elusive,
the slant of his shoulders in worn tweed
softened by sun as you half-rise
from your Café Brea table to stop him,
reduced to his language. Another
mistaken identity: all the young men
with thin shoulders turn and rapidly
walk away. But in the story, he looks
for you and finds you, before losing you again.

Maybe you're long past those miles
of grief and worry. The *café au lait*
steams. And, after all,
you're enjoying your cigarette
and the unseasonable warmth that flushes
the Luxembourg's riches outside its gates.
Small joys that repeat themselves
when the larger joy no longer
coats the world with its tremble of color.

The telephone will have the last word.
And even if you know this city
too well, and go down certain streets
more fearfully than the fire-eater at Pompidou
thrusting flames in and out of his body,
think of the end of the story:
your lover, with one backward glance,
stricken; but you
deeper and deeper into the luminous core.

Choices

"If suicide is allowed, everything is allowed."
Ludwig Wittgenstein

I don't imagine you were considering
the autumn sky, its anticipatory
depths, constellations scattered
across glare like vine maple leaves,
a throbbing punctuation;
or the forest, lacustrine, flooding
each side of the road. Nor
did you notice the air you breathed
as it rose from warm earth to marry
with the cold, the shock of it
in your nostrils, the brine.
Were the trees indifferent to you?
In the crowd of regrets that clogged
your ears, rushing up, plunging,
with nauseating speed, down,
you noticed no dialogue but your own.

You would have had no thought
for the consciousness behind the steering
wheel of a car, the breath
of a man, younger than you,
perhaps, coasting the county
road, its carefree curves,
toward lamplight, supper with his family,
a welcome of noise. Or a woman driver,
exhilarated, speeding home from her best
job yet, joy frosting her breath
as she sings. And what if,

                    what if
the driver has a passenger beside him
on the seat, a child he's picked up
from an after-school game, a boy
with perfect vision, the whites
of his eyes calm as shells with
a knowledge the very young
scarcely recognize in themselves?
Who sees you step out from the roadside
before you actually do so,
sees, with the intuitive quickening
of an animal, in the set of your head,
the hunch of your shoulders, the intention
you haven't yet fully formulated.

He hears his father shout.
The car stalls, judders, headlights
dipping. It rears, sentient
as a horse, swerves, stops dead.
They stay rigid, your collaborators,
unready for this particular election.

In a moment they will step out of
the car, the safe cave,
and bend over your body. They will turn
you over, your warmth escaping
from tweed like air from a tire.
The silence, the sigh
they will carry away with them
as they carry this night, this year

fastened to their shoulders like a yoke.
Autumn upon autumn it will press
its ridges into flesh and spirit,

until, years later, sleepless
in his old age, in an old house,
October's ambivalence pungent
at the window, the man who was the boy
remembers how the rain began, then,
inaudible as the breath of a newborn,
warm on their eyelids and heads,
how it spattered his father's face
as it lifted toward him, explicit,
transmuted in the car's headlights,
the crescents of his cheekbones luminous
and fragile as porcelain.

Little Fires: Camille and Gwen

1

"M. Rodin amuses himself by cutting off my income. . . I will be pursued all my life by the vengeance of this monster."

Camille Claudel, Letter to M. Lerolle,
c. 1913

"You tell me God pities the afflicted, God is good, etc. . . . Shall we speak of your God who lets an innocent rot in the depths of an asylum? I don't know how to keep myself from . . ."

Camille Claudel, Letter to Paul Claudel,
1929, from L'asile de Montdevergues

"Camille se suicidait à petit feu."

Paul Claudel, *Journals*

Outside is warmer.
Across the field poplars lean
like a row of women who have walked
in a line from the villages
to the grave of their sister.

My thumbs feel the corrugations
of their black clothing.
Maybe one is the mother, maybe she
can still remember
her daughter's face. The wind

ruffles the edges of my skirt.
It braids the chatter from the *pensionnat,*
the shrill, random voices,
into a stream, tames them

68

the way the rocks are tamed

and shaped by weather.
On the path where the old men pause
to spit and piss, the grass is yellow.
They stare, wordless, their
institution clothes flapping

about their stringy limbs, so light
the wind could lift them over the fields
like dingy kites, fly them
to the forgotten villages
of childhood.

Watching the clouds move, watching
the sheep move more slowly than clouds,
I am the stillest object. A spider
could wrap his threads around me.
Did I want one thing too much?

Does wanting one thing too much
break the world apart?
Mother, the doctor said I could
visit you, if you'd let me.
Let me. I'm afraid you might die!

A little corner of your hearth
is all I need, a pallet.
In my room the stone walls freeze my hands.
I've forgotten what it is to touch flesh.
When marble moved under my chisel

it came to life, clay flowed like menses.
I birthed a stone family.
Rodin stole them—he and his whore!
—O, I promise, I promise
to be calm! My fingers

curl in my lap, they are
little dead mice.
Against the wind the poplars huddle,
they are as old as I am. We have shed our excesses.
We are skeletons with hair.

Nearby, the men are digging potatoes.
The dirt clings to them from the nest
where the Mother potato
gives birth to her sweet, freckled children.
Inside their dark skins

the flesh is clean, it smells like clay,
like air from a country
I've been forbidden to visit.
When I put my nose
to their fresh cheeks, it is

like kissing. The sisters
give me a potato to bake
for supper. It crumbles
between my teeth, lavish as a breast,
each mouthful a giving.

2

"I may never have anything to express but this desire for an interior life."

Gwen John, Letter to Ursula Tyrwhitt

Gwen lies under the bushes
at the Villa des Brillants;
she has taken off her shoes,
she has taken off her cerise-colored *faille*.
All day she's walked the country lanes
leaving little packets of meat
for Tiger. The louts accost her.
When she calls, "Puss, puss," they leer.

Her head is light with hunger.
She dreams she's Robinson Crusoe.
She dreams she's beating brother Augustus
about the head. She beats and beats.
He smiles and smiles.

If she goes without love for a week,
she confesses, she freezes like a winter stream.
But Rodin mutters in his beard, "Immodesty
is not charming in a woman."

In Paris, on the Pont d'Alma, she is
prepared to jump. A gathering crowd
attracts a gendarme, and she climbs down.

News of Tiger drifts to Paris from Meudon;
she takes the train. Another series
of days searching and nights

naked under the bushes. When Tiger materializes
he's as skinny as she is.

Rodin, kind again, works on the head
of Whistler's muse she's been posing for;
he takes Gwen's head between his knees.

But in winter the Duchess returns.
Rodin won't see Gwen.
Gwen eats nothing but chestnuts
boiled in milk. The smell of food
sickens her. She's so thin
no one wants to draw her.

She draws herself, nude,
in front of the window. She draws herself
wearing a check skirt.
She draws Fenella, she draws Chloë.
She writes to Ursula, I want my drawings
to be definite and clean like Japanese drawings.

She has migraines, she has the grippe.
While modeling she faints.
She writes to Rodin, Love is my illness.
There is no cure but you.

Rodin sends her a basket of plums.
She eats two a day until they're gone.

Rodin dictates to Judith Cladel,
I always have flowers in the morning,
and make no distinction between them and my models.
Many flowers are women with their heads bowed down.

The anemone is only an eye, cruelly melancholy.
It is the eye of a woman who has been badly used.

Gwen writes, My visitor calls me,
His name is Solitude. He comes constantly in life.
I love him though he is cold.
He'll follow me till the last day.
But I know him well. I don't fear him.

A woman's head, dictates Rodin, has the softness
of a dog's eye. A spirit which becomes motionless
when the tyranny of passion has disappeared.
When passion is in control, she sucks like a vampire.

He adds, I have achieved a thing today
which I had not previously attained so perfectly—
the commissure of the lips.

Hawthorn

Maybe it fascinated him because
beside it behind the fence
waited the comely, taunting child.
Maybe he was mystified
when the flower, greenish-white,
turned pink and, two weeks later,
was crimson as fresh blood.

Maybe, when the taunting child,
years afterward, became his lover,
the tree seemed like their love,
the deepening colors, the thorns.
Thorns jutted from every branch,
from individual shoots
that clustered, pale green and tender.

I prune my hawthorn yearly,
before the shoots, grown numerous,
tangle high among old branches,
or ramble across the fence
into my neighbor's trees.
In gloves and heavy clothing
I start at the edge like the prince
approaching Sleeping Beauty,
and carve my way in.

The thorns tear my shirt,
penetrate my gloves, my shoes
when I step on lopped branches.
The older the limbs, the harder

their polished brown spines.
Inch-long and strong as steel,
they sting as if tipped in poison.

Cleared, the tree is angular and open;
its airiness invites the unwary.

What did he think, an old man,
when he saw the tree again?
Had his deft trimming cut to the heart,
baring its implacable framework?
Or had the limbs, untended, locked
into a thicket of swords?
This tree, so white and pink and blood-red
that fevered and beaded his skin
with a stigmata of perforations.

IV

Our Parents

I admit that their lives had those slights,
those undones, faults like missed threads
you find in the sheets they call seconds
we buy at sales and are assured by the clerks
who have been taught motherly firmness
and will swear on the company bible,
are just as strong, as lasting, and no one
will notice the unevennesses unless they look
closely (and who ever does in bed?). The colors
almost hide the flaws. And their lives were woven
together in such imperfections, an almost
primitive slub of carelessness or resentment,
a humdrum darn, never really forgotten however
ironed over, momentarily forgiven, to present
a rough kind of smoothness, except for the days
when truly large rents and a thinness
worried us. The selvedges were skewed.

In the backyard we play tent, hanging
the fabric over maple limbs, though
it's far too short to cover us. The bugs
are humming the washing-machine blues.
It's nice to be out here, out of that
tight-fitting union-suit of a house;
the air smells like distance. See,
you can see the light from the stars
sifting down through the holes, Morty.
They sting like firecrackers. It's fun,
isn't it? Though scary and a bit cold
and the mosquitos are too awful tonight
for us actually to be enjoying it.

Domestic Interiors

The music turns me round like Proust backtracking,
one phrase fuguing into another, a contra-
puntal thrust of infinite associations.
A table, eating soup, I muse out the window
at the undistinguished houses, the houses' cats
swaggering across the road, and let myself
be fiddled down the unexpected, though,
unlike Swann and Odette, I don't greet
when it comes round *la petite phrase de Vinteuil,*
the national anthem of their love. Proust
wouldn't say exactly if it were Debussy,
Saint Saëns or Franck. Right now I'm swallowing Fauré
with my soup. Involuntary memory dabbles
in my mind's tureen. For thirty years I've lunched
facing a window, watching neighbors change
their cars, their pets, their husbands, as noontime inched
past us: minestrone, *l'oignon,* cream
of tomato with goldfish crackers in it, the nose,
the palate savoring transcendental crumbs,
while music swirls its veils.

                    Helpless, I'm returned
to a blue porcelain kitchen table where I gape out the window
shocked at Roger and Jack Erickson's pale
bodies as they wrestle in their bedroom next door, naked
and furious as Cain and Abel. Replayed, the scene
where my mother interrupts her tirade to hurl a milk bottle
at my father who tries to laugh it off, secrets
of the bedroom a blue-white spatter. The plates dim,
the young trees lining the back fence pause in their growing,

as anguish seeps through the broken wall and through the sequence
of chords where innocence is lost and found and lost.
In a trice the heart stops, shifts gears, alters its direction.

Light glazes Mother's black-red Chinese bowl
in the cupboard behind me, the "don't touch" of the past,
my childhood interred in the sutured crack. Oblivion
lay in the arms of the lake, the glitter of sun
on the aspens, and with those silent angels, books.
Until the soft shock of memory breaks from the ordinary
and turns its laser onto the glacier floor,
melting the ice, exposing life preserved
entirely down to the last bone button.

                              Hearing
her name, the child opens her eyes, blood courses
through her frozen limbs. She steps into
her parents' arms for the withheld embrace. They sit
to the daily nourishment of music and soup.

Looking Back

I don't know what made me dream
you were a child again, except
finding that old photo in which
you're four years old and smiling,
eyes masked by the shadow
of your glasses, mysterious as a raccoon.

In my dream you're older
and the smile's become so knowing,
the folds of your mouth tuck it
primly in. Though I quailed and questioned,
you led me as if you were the parent
down an unlit hallway narrow as a foot-bridge
where I dared not look around
at cries and wrestlings, alarming
thuds from somewhere nearby.
Then, without warning, you were gone,
the way grown-ups suddenly leave
children they believe they have led
out of danger. And I woke up trembling,
the blind animal of my heart frantic.

Now you've sent me a poem from
my mother's house, about an old snapshot
taken when I was a child. You describe
my grandmother, mother, brothers
and me at a nameless lake.
You fit yourself into this cycle
of innocence and experience, trying

to interpret what the children's
veiled eyes conceal.

Sean, I would like to say
we're both safe on shore, beyond violence
or sorrow, that we protect each other
by the power of willing good—which is only
another way of naming love.

But I know better. The children's eyes
know better. They say the dark bridge
is always there; they say we must brave it,
child, mother, child; they say
looking back into each other's eyes
can steady us, the way
a paper boat is nudged and steadied
across a flooded creek-bed by someone
kneeling on the bank, holding a birch twig;
he leans out over the water, the wand
tight in his hand, which does not waver;
the vessel tips and then is righted,
rallying in the swell and spin:
for a moment even the birds pay attention.

A Sentimental Education

"O, schwester nimm den krug aus grauem thon. Begleite mich! den du vergassest nicht Was wir in frommer weiderholung pflegten."

Stefan George, *Jahrestag*

It was a good year for German opera.
The queen died, leaving the sad, handsome king,
leaving the goosegirl daughter
with her dirndles and skimpy braids,
leaving snapshots and jewels enough
to distribute to the servants.

The bomb had killed the dragons and trolls.
No one under the bridges now except
stepmothers and Fate.
Your George translations were
suitably sorrowful, but I
was not ruthless enough
to write novels.
We agreed that symbolism
had a few good years left.
Nevertheless, we both
had to have our
wombs vacuumed out; you twice.

It was a good year for Italian tenors:
on the other hand we adored lieder.
Your Papa married again,
a woman who sang in the choir.

When you took your orals the second time
you were madly in love.
We were addicted to the movies:
while the good girls got married,
the bad ones died, nobly.

 Circular arguments in my cozy
 red room or drying out on the beach
 where the lake was lukewarm
 and slightly polluted.

My brothers were back, thinner and more hairy.
In your stepmother's house the books
ceded to flowered wallpaper.
Luckily you had given me
the little ring your mother left
which didn't fit anyone else:
an eye without a twinkle.
We followed our lovers to large cities.

Ezio continued to belt out arias
from center stage while you
sat panting in the shadows.
Furnished rooms, unspecified incidents,
the I-don't-know-what-all
of public thoroughfares—
it would be romanticizing
to put it differently.
I still thought the paragraph
emotional, but your
posh boarding school had taught you
that ladies are neat.

Leading to the polite note
signed with both their names
like an RSVP, regrets
at having to miss
a boring party: that is,
the necessary euphemisms, that is,
plausible explanations, beautiful
penmanship, the very model of,
et cetera, so to speak . . .

The Uses of Exile

For my father, 1894–1977

"I feel that it is necessary to me, prescribed for me to be alone, an outsider, and alienated from every human context whatsoever."

"The city gives us the feeling of being at home. Cultivate the feeling of being at home in exile."

"The danger is not lest the soul should doubt whether there is any bread, but lest, by a lie, it should persuade itself that it is not hungry."

"It is necessary to uproot yourself. Cut down the tree and make a cross and carry it forever."

"Indeed for other people I do not exist. I am the color of dead leaves like certain unnoticed insects."

"Perhaps all that is not true. Perhaps all that is true."

Simone Weil, 1909–1943

"Let's discuss the question. Which side do you want to take?"

My father

If I mourn, May rains
are as responsible on steaming asphalt,
and not so much fresh-turned earth, as
city dampness, giant blooms
of exhaust confirming my urbanity,
as well as absences,

the missed exchange of looks, touch,
language. There's a white space
in me, something bleached.

Exiled, in a foreign city,
the year of your death,
I found that solitude
cures loneliness, acquired
lifelong companionship between
rue de Vaugirard and the gardens
where Ford, Léonie, and Caroline Gordon
used to walk; took my meals at
the Polidor, which knew James Joyce.

Simone read beside me
at the *bibliothèque;* we bent
to our books like robins or peered
at bookshelves, amiable giraffes,
glasses sliding down our
intellectual noses.
Preserve your solitude! she wrote.
Some days I didn't speak
three words in any language

but heard what the dust said
blown up the Metro steps where
the sweepers were on strike,
yellow tickets like yellow snow
or yellow stars clung
to my ankles. How not to be

political, the world's hand
on our shoulders, pushing us
earthwards; still,

I led a simple life
in a simple room, papered
with pink and yellow roses
reminding me of lives poets
are supposed to live.
Baudelaire in his garden salon
always wore a red rose placed
on his bust by the young
which we never were.

I did my homework a block away
from where that other Jewish woman's house
stood, plaqued for posterity,
her prose impeccably tailored
as her suits, cropped as her hair.
Some refugees eat well; none of us
take root; we wander
in that ash the mistral
blows across Europe.

I wrapped myself in your death
like Simone's old army cape,
muffled to the ankles, whittled down
by actual hunger and the kind
of starving those who dream
of angels with swords and fire
have, whatever season, country, dialogue
we're in; in caves of books our visions

thin us to the bone.

We cast spindly shadows on city streets,
estranged from everything: our poems,
our polemics, our own flesh and blood:
each spring the anniversary of the death
of the beloved. Only the smell of Paris
where you never were, a city man
who knew the U.S. like the palm
of your own hand, can bring you
lightly to your daughter's side.

You walked with us along
the streets of the Marais and in
the Jewish cemetery, that putrid corner
where they returned the bodies
of Abelard and Héloise,
an exile to the end,
a travelling man, Marx
in one hand, a Millay translation
of *Flowers of Evil* in the other.

Wandering Ishmaels, blown leaves,
stay near me, though you decline
to come down on either side.
You've given away the shirts
off your backs, your books,
your last dollar, and are
essential dust, refusing gravity,
arguing forever in thin air
over scoured ground.

I watch the city birds

fly out, abrasive and absurd,
swooping across the lawn,
hoping with grace or luck
to find one pure drop of water
on a blade of grass. Such sweet
nonentities. I swear
they never stop, but live,
somehow, in motion.

Northern Idylls

During spring break Debbie Schwartz and I would bike
from south Minneapolis to the boathouse near the U.
The water-soaked musk of the dock, the pungence of rotting

Enveloped in fog the rowboat with its three occupants
moves down river between stands of birch. The adolescent
boy gazes at the tree trunks glimmering like bodies which

When I lifted my paddle water would bead on the slender
blade. I'd lift and ply, lift and ply,
then backwater. A long, green leaf, the canoe would slide into

The boy is singing, dispensing notes the way
birds do, with a sort of mindless purity, while the men,
uniforms stiff with frost, flex their huge, red

There, the Mississippi was shallow and brown as amber.
Taking turns, we'd paddle, then ship our oars and remove
our shirts. In minutes our breasts would sting as if

He is singing Hungarian folksongs. At the camp, the soldiers
discovered he could sing. They discovered his voice the way
they discovered jewelry sewn into the lining of the clothes of

One night, in rowboats, two to a pod, we eased out onto
Lake Calhoun, our voices like thrown matches, flaring
and dying. Leon rowed me, his hair metaphysical, his

Though they can't understand the words, they hum the tunes.
The one with the scar thinks of Liszt. He imagines he's in Venice,
he imagines his gondola is drifting toward the hotel where his lover

After Edna and I left the Rosens' dock, the wind
came up. We were entangled in reeds. We rowed for hours,
muscles aching, until, luckily, Squish discovered the missing

The boy's voice falters as if he has forgotten or remembered
something. In their damp uniforms the men shiver. The boy's
cheeks are blanched, mottled as birchbark, with the cold or

Voices raucous with insults and laughter, my father and Moishe
   Rosen
argued politics, oars waving, while we kids threaded our lines
with angleworms to hook sunfish and perch or bullheads as black
   as

Shouting, the soldiers prod the sly-faced peasants,
and demand eggs or newly butchered meat for the officer's table.
They flourish their pistols while the boy drags sacks reeking of

How I loved those summers on the lakes and rivers, imagining
I was Sacajawea or Evangeline, gliding down waterways
or through the bayous in melancholy search for my lost

Attention! They sit up straight, they button their collars.
Good soldiers. They will make the boy row on the way back up-
   stream.
His voice pierces the fog, while sleet scours the freshly dug

Archaic Couple

Sarcophagus, fired clay, Cerveteri, c. 520 B.C.

Their bodies gleam,
she leaning lightly against
his warmth, one arm supported by some cushions,
he, bare-chested,
solid, a prow or figure-
head of the couch they lounge so gaily on. The

disposition
of their hands gives their cheerful
informality a form, as if music
played around them,
as if they'd just put down their
own instruments or would, in a moment, rise,

lift pipe and lute
and move into the room toward
us, their friends, to join the dance. His right arm curves
about her neck
to rest on her bare shoulder,
hand cupped as if to receive or to let go

what's been freely
given. But his other hand,
palm up, is open as a water-lily.
Her left hand is
under his, and may have held
a vessel, a piece of fruit, a plover's egg.

But her right hand,
two fingers bent, two straight, signs
ancient mysteries, a spell to thwart evil

or reaffirm
conjugal vows. How could this
couch be a death bed? Their features are replete

with love, polished.
Is the sculptor showing us
how they'll be in after-lives, handsome and young,
before stale days,
before the body's diminished,
before the smile's turned tentative, or sour?

Roped off, the warm
pink glaze of flesh eludes us.
We suffer the lazy challenge of their stare,
coveting that
athletic happiness. We
wonder if we were so arrogantly sure.

Did we, ending
a summer day, our canoe
beached, rising from our bed of wild grass, smiling
like these lovers
in archaic innocence
at an unmarred world, truly coupled, relaxed

hands joined, did we,
dear one, imagine, stepping
from earth toward water, plunging into that cold
flood as if it
were a miraculous stream,
that our love, vitrified by fire, could cheat time?

July 1990

Seaven Teares

(for Broken Consorts)

Not to put too fine a point on it,
the two had entered the most terrible
intimacy of love and suffering, admitting

no other correspondent save the Invisible
Third who hovered in whatever room
their intentness gathered. They sat opposite

each other in big chairs, he, eyes closed,
listening to his body's messages, she,
observing him from behind her book's camouflage,

spying out the minutest detail of change.
The looking, listening, became a total act.
Beyond the living-room's sealed window, time

and snow fell, white transparencies,
as she reviewed their calendar, weight
sifting from his bones, an insubstantial drift.

One evening, startled from her book, she saw
he'd metamorphosed into the lover she'd known
thirty years ago, the bow of his collar-

bone, the pedicel neck and, in the lamp's
aura, fine features articulate and a boy's blue gaze.
She beheld the essence of the man, the self

unclothed, pure spirit, the shed flesh revealing,
like the inscape of a winter plant, his scaffolding.
How they concentrated on this doing and undoing,

this raveling dance, while their thoughts furiously crisscrossed
the charged room, sparked, then crackled with the bonfire
of her focus on him, his focus on becoming other.

She watched his swollen hands, turned smooth and slender,
finally compose. After the last kiss, she slipped
from his chill finger the once-embedded ring.

May 1991

Changing Places

For Nick and Robin

In the shower I step back and my foot
presses something soft that gives.
My heel remembers

the high room, the piles of boxes,
books stacked, clothes heaped
on the bare floor. And scuttling among the debris
my grandson Nick, small legs
pushing him crabwise on his bottom
as he eyes the detritus of moving.

He watches his father, his uncle, their friend
dismantle his bed, take down
his music boxes, his hanging birds.
He gazes up through stalks of legs
at aunt, mother, grandmother
sorting, packing.
Offers of Cheerios or cheese
fail to distract him. He scoots underfoot,
gentle, a breakable we carefully
step around, until I,

clearing out the linen closet,
step back and feel under my shoe
soft stuff like a rag. And, looking down,
see his hand, pink and pillowy as a starfish,
trapped under my heel.

I gasp and Nick's face crinkles.
All the long day's uneasiness

coalesces into pain, immediate and physical,
expressible. He screams.

I ache to hold him, but it's his mother
he needs, and she scoops him up
and presses him to her. Body to body
clings, Nick a limpet, a sweet pulse.
Gold head to gold head. The objects
of his life removed, the room denuded,
the safe home dispersed into thin air,
are for a moment forgotten as he finds

his first and real place. He puts his
tear-smeared mouth to his mother's breast
as they sit on the dusty floorboards.
I yearn toward that rare, healing solace,
as flesh comforts flesh, conjoined
against the sea of change, the battering tides.

Black Pottery

Black pottery, you say, has nothing to do
with you or me, has nothing, you say,
smiling across your stack of papers
and open books, references, dictionaries,
nothing to do with anything.
What they left, used, buried with the dead,
there is no living language to describe,
merely these jars and urns, crude dishes,
the commonplace, the quotidian.

In my dream, they showed me the half-eaten corpse
of a cat splayed in a box, rotting.
And I felt death's wrinkled hand squeezing
my womb. I dug among piles of rags
and colored cloths to find the one warm cloth
that might revive it. When I picked it up
in the wrapping and held it against my breast
I felt a breath begin.
The animal became a warm, sucking child.

The wife hands the husband a fruit, an egg,
a dish, and, above the doorway of the hall
two leopards flex their haunches, tensile as bows.
Women dance in a flurry of scarves and skirts.
Young men wrestle, their curved torsos
straining. In red paint, the two-headed lion
with the serpent's tail, his second head that
of a sinuous-necked horned ibex, rears
on the black canopic funeral urn,

exciting terror in their hearts, and joy.

Approaching Malpensa

"There is Auschwitz, and so there cannot be a God."

"I don't find a solution to this dilemma. I keep searching but I don't find it."

Ferdinand Camon, *Conversations with Primo Levi*

1

Each in our own space we doze,
anonymous parcels in a cryonic cargo
destined for a planet not yet mapped.
When I raise the curtain I see
clouds unfurl in rivulets like
wind-blown or water-blown sand.
The roar of the plane is oceanic
as we migrate toward Malpensa.

Do we choose or are we chosen?
"Strawberries, strawberries, ten cents a box,
Jew-baby, Jew-baby, pull up your socks,"
the boys taunted, chasing me home from school.

"What's a Jew?" I asked my mother,
the secular, divorced radical.
"Who was Jesus?" "Why,"

asks Camon, "did you let them
recognize you as a Jew
instead of a partisan?"
Levi replies, "They told me
if you're a Jew, we send you
to Carpi-Fossoli, if you're a partisan
we stand you up against a wall

and shoot you. But also," he adds,
"I wanted to show them
that even Jews can fight back."

In a dream I come to the house
where I live and can't get into:
someone has locked the doors
and glued newspaper over the windows.
I scurry from side to side
like a hunted animal, pounding
the walls, crying to my daughter
to let me in. A corner of newspaper
is lifted and she looks out.
"You can't come in," she says.
But it's not her face
that stares at me. Pale, scrunched-up
with malice, it's my face
peering through the glass.
When at last she opens the door,
I sob, "Why did you lock me out?"
"Because I felt like it,"
my own self answers, smirking.

2
In a Turin café, the men resume
their conversation, amid sounds
of shouting and curses; a gang
of roughs outside is being shoved
against a wall and patted down
by police. "Don't you ever
feel anger or desire for revenge?"
asks Camon. Levi shrugs.

"I'd say my lasting curiosity
about Germans excludes hatred.
I'm trying to understand."

Trying to understand, four years ago
I bypassed fabled palaces
and scanned the Venetian map
for the Jewish section.
I dragged my daughter through streets
so hot only cats sidled through,
empty of sound or motion. A plaque
on a building commemorated the rabbi
who had gathered his flock around him
when the Fascisti gunned their trucks
through the quarter. Leaving silences,
we came to a small piazza
where men strolled or talked in groups.
For tourists there was a flea market—
a poor showing: cracked cups and wrinkled
paperbacks. Catching the light
like jewels shone military buttons,
an iron cross, armbands with swastikas,
photographs of Mussolini.

Later, in Florence, we looked down
from the Boboli gardens and saw the city,
a womb of red and gold. We ate pizza
under acacia trees that had sheltered
intriguers from the Pitti Palace.
The Duomo rose before us in the haze,
the intact virgin mother brooding

over her children. All week
an armed police van parked
in front of the locked iron gates
of the synagogue on via de'Pilastri.
We ate in the kosher restaurant
next door, on Good Friday.

3
We're floating now, floating
above Milan in such a warm
blue sea you feel as if
you could swim in it forever,
though thin patches of white
on the surface remind me
of the frozen lakes I skated on
in Minnesota, in my fearless days
when I believed I was light as a bird.

O, I could have grown up
Bathsheba Yarmanelski
if the immigration officer had understood
my grandfather. Or I could have been
a Joan Marguerite, if my grandmother
hadn't scared my mother into altering
the names on my birth certificate,
initialling me for Ben Zion,
the great great rabbi grandfather
from Königsberg—to keep his memory green.

If our names choose us like our bones,
we're framed, defined for life,

our big toes tagged for the coroner.
All is circumstantial. "There are different ways
of being a Jew," says Levi. "Auschwitz

was my real university."
"What was it like," Camon asks,
"hearing Hitler speak?" Levi,
the scientist, deliberates:
"It was like the forming of a mutual induction
between a cloud charged with electricity
and the earth. It was
an exchange of lightning bolts."

4
We approach the long stairway,
the ladder to earth. Few of us are thinking
of fatal plunges down stairwells.
For a frozen moment we remain
countryless, without status
state or culture. In the suddenly
stultifying compartment, sans air-
conditioning, we pack away our books,
our bad thoughts with the good,
ready to hit the ground,
carry off our carry-ons,
start the scavenger hunt;

universal tourists searching for
God knows what, a place, a deity,
lost civilizations. Memories
and names we never had.

Somewhere along the line
we must pass through customs,
show our passports, true or false,
declare ourselves. Breach the borders.

V

Our Children

Even in the womb they stir uneasily,
waiting for Never; then forget,
forgetting again as love awakens them
with a kiss and a gun.
       Although halcyon days
are only half days half the time,
light coming and going like offspring.

But the door-slam that jars you
in your brown study sets off
white sparks; your spirit shudders
like your door, scarred with their hard
shoes, threats, exquisite vocabulary.
       Wanting to get out yourself,
you yell, "Then, get out!"

and the use of it savagely
bites your lip; your eye remembers,
scalding. Adrenalin achieves the heart's
half-hearted desire.
       O, what a roll-back
of memory, what a series of Saturday
afternoon comic disasters, your own
not-so-silent cinema of frustration,
the nurture of anger, revenge,

ingenious escapes.
       A line unravelled
as you pushed away from the shabby
dock of childhood, scarcely able
to control the surprisingly unwieldy

rudder. And wind, wind, is what you
prayed to the world for.

In the long run
you accept the price of admission
and, with renewed lung power, shout
for another round, lap, bowl, innings,
chance to do it all over again,
chance to taste it.

The Clearest Expression
of Mixed Emotions

"At least it's poetic, the autumn is really beautiful. . ."

Astrov, *Uncle Vanya*

Take the longest of our encounters, or the shortest:
in the corridor outside the classroom, or on the grass
after a performance of *Cyrano* or *Uncle Vanya.*

The night was foundering in mildness; it pressed
against our mouths, our eyes, like lips. The season
was late spring or early autumn, each leaf

falling in such a slow spiral, it was as if
our mutual friend, hidden on the trapeze over the stage
where Cyrano lay dying, dropped them. Uncle Vanya

murmured last lines to Sonya who, kneeling, wept.
For us, the campus grounds in Gothic shadow
were part of the plot, and the wild rabbit that paused

in the moonlight indicated romance, though
the buildings were designed for the heroic:
leaving for wars or returning from them. Something

inevitable, though human. We strolled across
that skillfully lit place, indigenous as ghosts
floating through the flesh of our successors.

Who would think to ask us weighted questions,
actors in such light costumes? It was just
a casual summer evening at the theatre

before we went our separate ways, walking
off or boarding the yellow street-car with
its circus gaiety that clanged across

the deserted town. Was it the archetypal
snowfalls that made our silences heraldic
before we learned the language of that country

particularly distinguished for its elegies,
its epiphanies, its elastic vocabulary
anyone can say or understand?

Getting the Picture

As usual at the gallery I have to put my nose close
to the painting and remove my glasses in order to see
the artist's name and his brush strokes, or the exact detail
of etchings. I back away to appreciate the relation
of space to object. Further back, still, for the whole
picture, that is, the quintessential view,

if there ever is one. I remember learning to sew, my view
of the needle's eye. Holding thread and needle close
to my face, I could see the little groove inside the hole
like the hollow of my own eye, and peering, could see
the strands of silk twisted into one strand, the relation
of tongue to groove, the fit of things. But detail

loses its charm. Desire lay beyond mere detail
to the grandeur of the completed garment, the flattering view
of myself. And basting over and over bore no relation
to that vision. Why those miles of stitches had to be so close
and even, though in the end no one would see
them, my mother despaired of teaching. I loved, whole-

heartedly, consummations. Drawing, I filled a whole
page with the hieratic head Leo brought in. The details
bored me, though the rest of the class labored to see
exactly lips ears eyes. Like the scenic versus the dramatic view
dear to novelists: Proust, seeing Albertine's cheek so close
he could count her pores, stepped back, and the relation-

ship foundered. It's a murky subject, the relation
of emotion to distance. Apprehending the scene whole
lofts it to the realm of the abstract. But how terrifying close-
ups are! When Caroline specified three details

for every scene (see Flaubert, see Chekov) that short view
turned me poet. But when I take off my glasses to see

you and me in this old snapshot, my myopic squint sees
only the enormous stretch of sky and water and our relative
smallness on the rocks. Hard to tell whether the view
is of us or the lake; we make a deceptive whole.
In spite of the brilliance I can't make out the details
of that summer, the mountain of particulars we were too close

to relate to. As if one wished the apple whole
having bitten it, I step back to see, to obliterate the details
that blocked the view and, by doing so, lose it. As the shutters
   close.

The Miracle

When she was sure that what she saw,
steadier than reflections in the pond,
more solid than the village sycamore,
was the unbelievable
dressed in its real wings,
she ran to get the neighbors.

White dust danced in the plaza
and the dwarf church glared.
All at once their hands
hung out of their sleeves like spades
and the sleeves scraped their wrists:
they were the looked at;

though the six of them stared
until earth and sky fused
and the town behind them floated
in time, in timelessness,
as the vision hardened
beyond translation.

Which of them could report exactly
what each had seen differently?
Though that something was seen
became their monument.

Even the grandchildren coming after,
irritated by these scraps of blurred memory,
as disappointing as exposed film,
believed, because they had to.
And the town became famous;
tourists pried cobbles from the street.

As for the apparitions, they
avoided the sacred spot.
They hung around the orchards, where lovers,
among fallen peaches,
brushed them off their faces, like gnats.

Euclidean Walk

(Homage to Magritte)

1
When is an easel at ease? When it is glass,
when it is easily seen through, beyond
the wall of a room, which is sky, clouded.

When is a tower, a road? When, empty,
except for us, it ascends to the vanishing
point in sky, clouded.

The curtains open or close upon a view
that changes your life, ideally,
since the view is bereft of ideas.

We can go from corner to corner
without ever reaching the real horizon,
if there is one. The ideal painting

may be the unreal one, transparent as glass,
on an easel manifestly solid, or so
the painter pretends. Or is there

no somewhere, after all,
but only an infinity
of views?

2
The road is not a tower because
two figures stand on it in some
sort of relationship we can't see

seeing as how we look down
on them from inside the tower. The painter
placed them there with the arrogance of God.

But we are human and care with a
moody understanding. They have been thrown down
with a flick of the wrist, and you and I,

here by chance, observe them and speculate
upon their meaning. The road ends
in a point as sharp as the apex of a tower,

at which all things disappear.
We are silent about death.
We speak, in veiled terms, of love.

Communication from Planet X

Suddenly it occurred to us we hadn't heard
from you for some time, so we thought we'd send
a signal. Of course, our attention span is short,
unlike yours, and so we spin from thought
to thought, unthinkingly as it were. Still,
your signal, though quite weak, was noticed, a faint
yellowish-pink pulse on someone's screen, and therefore
on all of ours, since we're not divided as you are
by space and time. We wondered if you perhaps had
stopped receiving and so stopped sending. Though which
is which is a distinction we hardly make since communication
is reciprocal. But you see, the lack of your signal

has been noticed by that which we might perceive (if that's
the word) as a blankness (if there is such a condition
without time or space). We merely wondered when
(if there is a when) you might send what we formerly
recognized as rather more than a blip, that stirred us
to respond in a range of color and speed, a sort of
meteoric shower as it were, reminding us
of heat and light, reassuring tremors or shifts
of whatever elements mysteriously recharge us.
In short, what we (to put it as delicately as possible)
would like to know (if one can call it knowing) is,
are you still there (wherever, of course, "there" is)?

Philosophical Investigations

*"Just don't pull the knot tight before being certain that
you have got hold of the right end."*

Ludwig Wittgenstein,
Notebooks 1914-1916

1

I've sanded my fingers so they'll sting when the right numbers click.
The heart of the vault goes on humming, invulnerable.

Your smile, a white knife, defends its drop of intention.
"If a lion could talk, I could not understand him."

Words, words, I've hunted for the uneven borders of your country.
Can love be defined? Is it or is it not a necessary truth?

Is your chair the sum of its parts? Are you a simple fact?
A room with two in it can close like a single eye.

Guessing at thoughts—a game. I usually lose.
Here's a penny in exchange. Bite it to see if it's real.

2

"The spirit of the snake and the spirit of the lion is your spirit.
It is only from yourself you are acquainted with spirit at all."

Tell me, does God speak to you? I can't hear him.
I'm of the tribe whose visions thinned us to the bone.

My pen snakes through my fingers before I can learn its tongue.
I can't get my kicks from the nuances of the particular.

Brother Jacob kept an account book of ladders and angels.
If I saw a light it would fall through the net of my words.

Yes, it is the indefiniteness we mourn.
We stand on the ground and watch it blink toward a foreign country.

3

In the glass case it was the sentences that sparkled and enticed me.
You could snap them like whips or break them into delectable morsels.

Looking back, I see the houses I built melting in the sun.
My ankle's scraped raw from dragging the chain of the world.

You don't need a map to plot the curvature of space;
where there is no meaning the fallen angel squats.

How mysterious the character of language! Its shifting surfaces!
It spreads and curls on the sea, an infinite oil.

"Where our words suggest a body and there is none,
there, we should like to say" *must say* "is spirit."

4

This island began with the two of us, we were only bodies.
Our presences filled the whole of space, like God.

A stone, the body of a beast, your body, mine,
sway in time like saplings, a level grove, a row of syllables.

I created the idea of you, and you turned solid.
You and I sit opposite like chessmen in black and white squares.

Be happy. I will it. My will creates the world.
Here is a collage of stars and rivers; I tear it from my side.

Being here is no crime; wanting more may be.
"God is how things stand. How things stand is God."

Only when I drop pen and paper do I hear day breathe against the window.
I wrote its silver motion; now, it opens the room like a key.

Circling Back

I walk here. Not every day.
This day the subject of the color
of plants presents itself,
having waited its turn,
mild and unrelieved of movement
like the lake which breathes, barely awake,
drawn in on itself, making
no motion toward sky or shore
or the houses fading behind trees,
the houses which are neither
the nervous gestures of Schiele
nor Sisley's nests, but glass
vessels clouded with moisture
like the sky which has invented
a color to match the gulls'.

But the plants, the plants
wait to be said. And I cannot
say the color they are
that is not yellow and not
green and not brown
and not white, that is not
ivory like the beaks of the black coots
and not snowy like the underwings
of the widgeons. They reject the gulls'
gray that on this day has
no light in it. Nor is there light
from the sky to pry open
the lake's eyelid and burnish
the mallards' verdigris necks.

This particular unshined gold,
unrich, unwarm, these bleached stems
that are my lattice for looking through
at what's left of the year,
are neither ice nor fire,
are what I'd like to think of
as the irreducible core
were the world somehow burnt-up
or frozen over; and these fronds,
branches, scoured limbs
stand here to be taken
for whatever the heart needs most
to resume being.

Dreams and Fables

We think we can make the old stories new.
Don't simply recount, I tell my students,
look for a different meaning in the tale.

Last night in a dream I saw you in a low,
cluttered room, turned away from the dark and raging
man who clamored behind you. Suddenly

he rushed forward, scattering chairs
and lamps, a furious, blind whirl, unstoppable
as a runaway stallion, rearing upon you.

You heard him and spun around, back to the counter,
the blooded globe of his face a hurled
boulder in the thick disorder of that hovel.

And I awoke sweating, certain of your danger.
Or was I the one who stood at the sink,
head bowed and fearful? Or was it I who attacked,

a winged fury? Was I both rage
and innocence at once? Rose White, Rose Red,
a malignant power, hand raised to strike

and destroy myself? Dear girl, you do not
belong in that scenario, humorous, cool,
a distant brightness. I've framed that place,

brick by brick, low ceiling, walls,
the changing-room where I repair
to address my demon, the dark, my angel.

Lakewold

You may suppose you have hooked a big one, sitting
in the boat for hours in your Mexican hat,
the jiggling bobbles shadowing your eyes.
Or cast from the shore in the evening, looking
for the one pink water-lily among the commoner
white ones. Once, a word dropped casually
from the mouth of your friend seemed to weight your line
and you saw the cork dip. Other times you surveyed
the hook dripping algae with the amused smile
of an expert who knows that only unexpectedly
will the occasion rise to what has been in your mind
a white threshold of perfectly arched portal
which you alone, handling the silver catch
or saying the magic phrase, this time mouthing it
as if you actually knew what it meant,
might jar open. To what you have no idea.

Because it reveals only the outer dooryard
of some as yet unproffered precinct which the householder
has designed in secret over a period of years.
Say, a knot garden or a topiary, a scree or a parterre
where only white plants are grown, woodruff, trillium,
artemisia. Nothing to excite excursioners,
such as a maze. But whether it offers a glimpse
of the lake through the thinned alders from the gazebo
placed expressly for one's pleasure, is only
speculation. On the warmest days you can detect
the scent of an unreachable blue from where you sit,
dissatisfied, under the ancient, damaged trees.

Lies, All Lies

*"It is a matter of knowing whether real life is in what one
does or in what one thinks of one's actions."*

Denis de Rougemont,
Dramatic Personages

1

In the long run, though, it's small matter
what happened or what didn't. For what one imagines
happening is equally true. Whether we were
participants or witnesses is perhaps mere semantics.

Did you or I stand on the bridge and give orders
directing events, or, off in a room
on the studio lot, were we writing and writing,
sending off page after page in sealed

manila envelopes? And so engrossed in our plot,
the wonderful swerves, coy changes, U-turns
and doublings-back, we didn't consider,
had no time for, what others made of the story?

Draw back. The heat of the moment has cooled.
A spark here and there. A crackling. Dénouements
soothe both actors and audience. We come down from heights,
eyes a bit damp, clutch our hankies. It's time

to think of midnight snacks, quick or long kisses,
moves. Though not much time, really, is left
to shift scenes. Not everyone's up to it. Beginnings
are difficult this far along in the day.

2

And old scenes dissolve as fast as new ones unfold:
that time we got lost in the snow, snowflakes on our mouths.
Those tears in the bedroom, fights in the car, making love
in an orchard, apples dropping like hours. Places

we dreamt or merely visualized while reading—
was it Tolstoy or Mann? When books were more real than life,
characters more familiar than our friends and lovers.
It happened. It did not happen. Ask me no questions.

Details blur. We were there; we were not there. *I saw you,*
you say. But I can't remember that time. *But you said,*
I say. You don't remember those words. Who were we?
Two others, now dead. Monsters. Angels.

3

Lies, all lies. Those lives twanging like strings,
note after note, blending and weaving
streams of music the ear can't retain. In its spiral
an echo plays hide-and-seek like a child.

Tears dry. The bed's made. We disperse. On the boards
sit chairs, waiting. In no time we'll see bodies in them,
hear voices resume. Our bodies? Our voices? Who knows.
Let's begin, then. Here's the first page.

VI

Private Showing

"One feels, but what one feels is comparable to certain photographic negatives that show only black until one puts them close to a light . . ."

Marcel Proust, *The Past Recaptured*

1

Do you see them side by side, the young woman
and the child? Young, you can tell by her *taille,* the slender
waist, the way she twists sideways against
the wind, the child a miniature version turning
toward her, her skirt, too, skimming the path.
And the river, agitated, brownish white.

The child's hand is flung outward like a scarf,
as if the wind were lifting it as well,
both caught in the reflections that eddy across the road.
Whether they're leaving or approaching the three-arched bridge
is anyone's guess. The basket on the woman's arm
tilts, full or empty. All that movement stilled,

repeating itself, like the story of the wet street,
how it slants back and back until lost in the V
of a mysterious brume, a *clair-obscur* blue-brown
that recedes beyond the round-roofed cart pulled
by a donkey. I imagine the clip-clop of hooves disturbing
this Sunday mood, a swish of wheels through puddles,

where what's indistinct is good to the impressionist memory:
the blurred edge of buildings, the tousled headdress of trees,
soft roofs, a smear of clouds in such wide buffets
across the sky you can't tell which is moving.
Is the story finished or just beginning? The child
is captured in the immediate which seems eternal.

2

The trees are never going to become old trees
in their girlish queue, fluttering toward the same
inverted V, that first principle of perspective.
Talk about blues and browns, autumnal hues,
calling up the smell of rain like blue umbrellas.
Forget your wet feet, the chill. There's a comfortable old donkey

brownness here, indefinite depths of *tristesse*
one must be young to fathom, although the young
move fast, discarding moods like clothing. Sprawled
before a fire with drink and book, you wonder how much
of this you meant to retain, if any, like a
fading tattoo that's seeped into your bloodstream

carrying bugs from a dirty needle, someone else's
plasma, a malaise. Does the past, however charming,
undermine us, siphoning away energy? Such picturesqueness!
The child leans into its mystery; the mother
probes intimations of despair. The curious journalist
would like to know if this is an important memory

or only another bad reproduction on your desk,
flat as a book, exposed to hindsight by lamplight.

3

Here I pause and shake out those saved woollies
which I've found, alas, hole-ridden, acrid with camphor.
And the sky outside my window is in flattest gray
after weeks of rain. And so I dress myself

in gray, although the trees persist in trotting out
brash pink, frail in the wind, petals scattered
before the flowers are fully opened in this temperate

climate of middle-age where it never gets
so cold you could die from it or so hot you sweat.
Still, like the journalist, one searches for

provenances, as if all one needed was
the authoritative stamp, the butterfly signature
recognized among scratched cobbles or scribbles
of branches, smears of graffiti, ravellings
that satisfy, the writing around the edges
that shows that someone lived here, loving the colors

and the bad weather. Though who knows what he left out
or painted over, wincing at the unexpected.
Whether the two figures were stroked in for comparative values
to suggest somewhat the proportion of the whole, the human
measured against nature's size, or if they were an actual
recollection and supposed to indicate truisms

about the relation of mother to child, the way the child
is leaning toward her, the way they both are leaning
blown by unseen winds, doubtless he meant it
to be casual, a genre painting, nothing
to *épater* the *bourgeois,* merely a rendering
of his own nostalgia for *plein air,* touched-up in the *atelier:*

the solitude of childhood under a cold sweep of sky.

4
Here are the blues and browns seen through several
pairs of eyes, the child's, her back turned
to the room in which the picture hangs, the woman's,
inside of whose mind the child vaguely dreams,
and the eyes of that cool other asking what it means.

For to be afraid of asking is to be lost
in the commuter's fog of terminal quiescence, doomed
to the tense present. The gathered shadows stay gathered
but the eye that sees them proposes a world of changes,
lightening or darkening the scene, conjuring up
a mélange of seasons, some never before remarked.

Seeing, also, in the glass that guards the surface,
itself, cloudy and foreign, backed by the mutable,
the room's quixotic clutter, the window's transformations
that insist on clashing with the fixed calm we long
so much to drown in. Still, this water color
has no real depth; we bob to the surface

buoyed by our own histories.

5

                       Let's say my parents
bought this picture on their honeymoon, moved it
from house to house, north to south to north,
an artifact more stable than the myth of their marriage.
As a child I gazed at it, when the windows were clouded
or what lay beyond them frightening, sometimes with tears.

Behind me moved my mother, her restlessness
altering the values, deepening or obliterating color.
And now, once more, it hangs on my wall, a failed
icon, seeping resonances like moisture.
Am I trapped in the intricacies of its Victorian frame?
Or unfettered, bridleless, do I eddy at random through years,

a ghost traversing a dim gallery, sleep-walking
in time's museum? Suppose one day a dark room
brightens, suddenly illuminated, like a window
high up in a deserted house, lit from the interior
by unseen hands. For an instant there's an *éclaircie!*
And I'm that child again, who, seeing double,

has been brought glasses that make two images
converge: the past merges with the present;
my nearsightedness is cured. I become both
child and woman, mother, daughter, and the painter
filling in his world. I accept this miracle
until the next showing. *Au revoir,* I whisper, *au revoir.*

See you in time's continuum, where I blunder,
translator of my own life, matching up memories
with meanings, scarcely interrupting my stroll before
moving on refreshed into the geography of the dream.
I adjust my lenses to bring far things near,
what's separate together. Seeing the dark clear.

Notes

"Dorothy" material gleaned from Dorothy Wordsworth's journals, *The Al-foxden Journal* and *The Grasmere Journals,* copyright © The Trustees of Dove Cottage, 1971, Oxford University Press paperback, 1973, 1974, ed. by Mary Moorman. I chose words repeated often in the text to use in a "concealed" sestina form.

"The Alphabet at Harar" refers to Rimbaud's poem "*Voyelles*" (1871), in which he assigns colors and images to each vowel. Harar is in Africa where Rimbaud worked as an export agent until he lost a leg to gangrene and cancer.

"A Desperate Enthusiasm." Anne Hutchinson was tried for heresy in Boston when she lectured on the meaning of scripture. She was banished and excommunicated. I'm indebted *to Divine Rebel: The Life of Anne Marbury Hutchinson,* by Selma R. Williams, Holt Rinehart and Winston, 1981, and historical documents for material.

"Schiele in Prison." Egon Schiele, the expressionist painter, was arrested for immorality and seduction because of his paintings. A judge burnt one in court. His father died of insanity caused by syphilis.

"Arachne" was changed into a spider by Athena, after boasting of her skill in weaving.

"Emily." I'm indebted to *Emily Brontë* by John Hewish, MacMillan and Co. Ltd., London, 1969; and to Mary Robinson's *Emily Brontë,* W. H. Allen and Co., London, 1883 (Robinson was Charlotte's friend). C. W. Hatfield's *Complete Poems of Emily Brontë,* Columbia University Press, New York, 3rd printing, 1952, was my source for the text of poems. Many other books including those by Phyllis Bentley, Muriel Sparks and Derek Stanford, Winifred Gerin, etc. were also provocative and helpful.

"Posthumous Letters." Kafka and his friends foresaw the fate of the Jews in Europe long before Hitler. He developed tuberculosis and spent the last years of his life in sanitoriums. His famous "Letter to His Father" never was given to his father, but was recovered and published by his friend Max Brod after both father and son had died.

"Marcel." In the voice of Proust at about the age of seven.

"Little Fires: Camille and Gwen." Camille Claudel, older sister of Paul Claudel, was a mistress of Auguste Rodin from 1883, when she was twenty and he was forty-one, until 1898. After their break, she became increasingly paranoid. She was committed to a mental hospital by her mother and brother in 1913, where she stayed until her death in 1943.

Gwen John, older sister of Augustus John, was a mistress of Rodin from 1903, when she was twenty-six and he was sixty-three, until around 1911. After their break, she moved to Meudon. He died in 1917. She died in Dieppe, in 1939, an indigent and ill from malnutrition, on her way to catch the ferry to England after the outbreak of the war. She was buried in a pauper's grave, site unknown. I am indebted to two books for information: *Camille Claudel, 1864–1943* by Reine-Marie Paris (Gallimard, 1984), and *Gwen John, 1876-1939,* by Susan Chitty (Hodder and Stoughton Ltd., 1984).

"Uses of Exile." Simone Weil was a young French philosopher and labor organizer, a Catholic convert who refused to join the church because of its exclusionary practices. She died of malnutrition, self-induced, in England, after being forbidden by the authorities to join the French soldiers fighting on the front. "Caroline" is Caroline Gordon, a novelist I studied fiction writing with; she was once a friend and secretary to Ford Madox Ford; Léonie Adams was a poet friend of hers and once a visiting poet at the University of Washington. A number of southern writers lived in Paris. Ford's apartment was on the rue de Vaugirard, across the street from the Luxembourg Gardens. "The other Jewish woman" is Gertrude Stein, who lived close by.

"Northern Idylls" is based on an episode from the documentary *Shoah.*

"Black Pottery" refers to Etruscan artifacts.

"The Clearest Expression of Mixed Emotions" is one of Auden's definitions of poetry.

"Euclidean Walk" is about René Magritte's painting of the same name.

"Philosophical Investigations" uses quotes from Ludwig Wittgenstein's journals of the same name, in which he questions some of his and Bertrand Russell's early conclusions about the nature of language, discussing its limitations in telling us how things are in the world.

"Private Showing." Thoughts on a water-color by an unknown impressionist painter.

More Copyright

Grateful acknowledgment is made to the following magazines for
  previous publication:

Akron Review: "For Sally in Paris."

The Arts: "A Desperate Enthusiasm."

Blue Buildings: "In the Hotel Garden"; "The Uses of Exile."

Blue Unicorn: "The Pastry Maker."

Crossing the River: "Country Boy"; "Looking Back."

Fine Madness: "Private Showing"; "Euclidean Walk."

Gilt Edge:" Dorothy."

Gettysburg Review: "Northern Idylls"; "Archaic Couple"; "Seaven
  Teares."

Hudson River Anthology: "Arachne."

Literature and Belief: "Circling Back."

Negative Capability: "Marcel"; "Little Fires"; "Felicia."

Pig Iron: The Epistolary Form: "Suspense at Meran."

Poetry Northwest: "The Clearest Expression of Mixed Emotions";
  "Undelivered Mail"; "Lies, All Lies"; "Our Parents."

Poetry: "A Sentimental Education."

Prairie Schooner: "Emily."

River City: "Choices"; "Domestic Interiors"; "Getting the Picture."

Seattle Review: "A Victorian Girlhood"; "Black Pottery."

Third Coast: "Communication from Planet X."

Yankee: "The Miracle."

The Best American Poetry, 1989: "Northern Idylls."

SeaPen Press: "Philosophical Investigations," 1977.

Beth Bentley was born and raised in Minnesota. She has a B.A. from the University of Minnesota and a master's degree from the University of Michigan in creative writing and English literature. She has lived in Seattle since 1952. Previous publications include *Phone Calls from the Dead* and *Country of Resemblances,* both published by Ohio University Press. Two fine press books, *Philosophical Investigations* and *The Purely Visible,* were published by SeaPen Press. She received a National Endowment for the Arts fellowship, and, after a year in France, has published numerous translations of contemporary French poets.

Colophon

This book was set in Garamond. It was produced on a desktop computer in Microsoft Word and PageMaker from Adobe Systems. The cover was produced in FreeHand from Macromedia.